*Persons Unknown*

Crab Orchard Series in Poetry
EDITOR'S SELECTION

# Persons Unknown

JAKE ADAM YORK

*Crab Orchard Review*

&

Southern Illinois University Press

CARBONDALE AND EDWARDSVILLE

13  12  11  10     4  3  2  1

The Crab Orchard Series in Poetry is a joint publishing venture of
Southern Illinois University Press and Crab Orchard Review. This
series has been made possible by the generous support of the Office
of the President of Southern Illinois University and the Office of the
Vice Chancellor for Academic Affairs and Provost at Southern Illinois
University Carbondale.

Publication was partially funded by a grant from the University of
Colorado–Denver.

**Crab Orchard Series in Poetry Editor: Jon Tribble**

Library of Congress Cataloging-in-Publication Data
York, Jake Adam.
  Persons unknown / Jake Adam York.
      p. cm. — (Crab orchard series in poetry)
  Includes bibliographical references.
  ISBN-13: 978-0-8093-2998-4 (alk. paper)
  ISBN-10: 0-8093-2998-0 (alk. paper)
  ISBN-13: 978-0-8093-8578-2 (ebook)
  ISBN-10: 0-8093-8578-3 (ebook)
  I. Title.
  PS3625.O747P47 2010
  811'.6—dc22                                    2010013040

Anyway, he stayed, watching the two creatures that struggled in the one body like two moon-gleamed shapes struggling drowning in alternate throes upon the surface of a black thick pool beneath the last moon.

\* \* \*

It seems like a man can just about bear anything. He can even bear what he never done. He can even bear the thinking how some things is just more than he can bear. He can even bear it that if he could just give down and cry, he wouldn't do it. He can even bear it not to look back, even when he knows that looking back or not looking back wont do him any good.

—WILLIAM FAULKNER, *Light in August*

# Contents

# Acknowledgments

Thanks to the editors of the publications in which some of these poems have appeared previously:

*Blackbird*—"And Ever"
*Cincinnati Review*—"Mothlight"
*Crab Orchard Review*—"A Natural History of Mississippi"
*Northwest Review*—"Self Portrait as a Moment in 1963," "Self-Portrait in a Plate-Glass Window," "Self-Portrait at a Bend in the Road," "Self-Portrait in the Town Where I Was Born," and "*Narcissus incomparabilis*"
*Shenandoah*—"Elegy"
*The Southern Review*—"Homochitto," "Darkly," and "Shore"
*Sou'wester*—"Sensitivity" and "City of Grace"
*Third Coast*—"Before Knowing Remembers" and "The Second Person"
*Yalobusha Review*—"The Hands of Persons Unknown"

"Darkly" and "Self-Portrait at a Bend in the Road" also appear as video poems, filmed by Steve Bransford at southernspaces.org.

With special thanks to Don Bogen, Garrett Hongo, Mary Flinn and the staff of *Blackbird*, and Jeanne Lieby and the staff of *The Southern Review*.

"Collect" appears as a limited edition broadside designed by Jan Murray of the University of Mississippi, for whom and to whom adequate thanks cannot be given.

Thanks to the judges of the 2008 Campbell Corner Poetry Prize, who recognized "Collect" as a distinguished entry.

Thanks to the editors of *Third Coast* and final judge David Wojahn for selecting "Before Knowing Remembers" as winner of the 2010 Third Coast Poetry Prize and honoring "The Second Person" as runner-up.

Thanks to the Regents of the University of Colorado for sabbatical leave during which this book was begun, and to the University of Mississippi for a residency that allowed me to complete this book.

Thanks to Jon Tribble for believing in this work, and to the staff of Southern Illinois University Press, especially Bridget Brown, Barb Martin, and Jennifer Fandel; and thanks too to Sarah McCartt-Jackson and Travis Mossotti for their help preparing this manuscript for press.

And to all my teachers, readers, and friends who have helped me find my way, especially Natasha Trethewey, Major Jackson, Ed Pavlic, Dan Albergotti, Harvey Jackson, David Keplinger, Dan Donaghy, Brian Barker, Maurice Manning, Ron Slate, Joshua Marie Wilkinson, Noah Eli Gordon, Joshua Poteat, Dave Smith, R. T. Smith, Claudia Emerson, Jeanie Thompson, and Sarah Skeen.

# ONE

# Homochitto

for Charles Eddie Moore and Henry Hezekiah Dee

In what language did it mean the river,

this tongue of rust
that gives the forest a name?

The trees can't tell you,

and the forest means you are alone
and a hundred years from Natchez

when the light begins to fold into the leaves.

Not even the birds can tell you.
Alone on the ruined wood

as Audubon saw them,
they can't even name themselves

so they disappear,

rising into the dusk,
their marks lost in early stars.

The painter could bring them down—
a brush of shot, then meteors of Latin—

*Picoides borealis, Campephilus principalis*
he could raise to that canvas heaven,

leaving only empty mouths
in the world below.

Swallows, starlings tongue the cavities
but cannot make the sound,

and the flickers offer only a syllable—
       *ki-ki-ki-ki-ki*—

invisible as the bird everyone is looking for—
ivory bill, lightning jag—

as if that call might end some other way.

As if, in one of a billion trees,
those wings

might cough from scarred wood
and write themselves back into history.

The trees are going now,
lost in the dark,

among them
the one you'll never find,

one side washboard-rough,
the other smooth as standing water

where two men were tied
one May night

to be beaten from this language.

A notebook, an informant's file
might tell the rest,

how he spotted them,
hitching out of Meadville,

how he waved them in,
fake badge flashing,

how he drove them off the map,

headlamps on the clay gash roads
and then the opened pith,

might record the vanished call—
                                    the *Kiwu!*
which means *Klansman, I want you!*

which means you are alone
and soon the water will take you

and keep everything but the names
nothing here remembers.

Now the trees give each other the wind
or the weight of some passing,

and every step stirs the forest's meal
into clouds of wings, moths

that tumble toward the river,
where they can semaphore like mayflies

or dragons on the lilies' hoods
or rise through the trees

to eat the night
from the brighter silk of day.

When the starlight's lint descends
the ground is fluttering.

Slowly it peels away
in innumerable blades,

each one a map of night
seen through water or leaves,

leaving a bolt,
hard and white as bone,

as if some bird had fallen
where those wings could feather it in quiet,

and around it, the shadow a body leaves,
the wake through which it falls.

Now the light is fine as dust.
The ground is cold,

rust-dark,
smooth as ash.

Somewhere there is a name for this.
Someone could write it down.

# Sensitivity

May 4, 1959

for Mack Charles Parker, lynched near Poplarville, Mississippi, April 24, 1959,
recovered from the Pearl River, May 4, 1959

Six weeks since that whisper rose
into the window of a stage
behind the Half Note's bar,
whisper Mingus let spread like a bruise,
*Lester Young is dead*, six weeks
since he fell from the sky,
dead off the plane from Paris,
and each night this goodbye's
gone more *sensitive*. Now
the flats are hid, and Handy's learned
to fold the sound of breath
inside his notes—the bleeding throat,
tongue's last epileptic flutter—
while Mingus thrills the bass
in waves of sound and fail
no microphone can hold.
Drinks tremble like the river
halfway from here to the grave,
pulled by wind or plummet,
cough of strings beneath the hand,
and uptown a tape is waiting
for magnets to say this again,
a teletype is writing a story
for tomorrow's *Times*—
a body pulled from a river
in Mississippi, with only fingers
for a name. Here
only the drinks are listening

as Ervin rises, ghosting Handy's lead,
and even they cannot hear
how the rivers heal their quiet,
how they fill their scars so perfectly
that remember feels like forget.
Then the breath is gone.
The wood hums a moment longer,
and each surface smoothes
till the glasses and the waters
are glass again and ready
to catch each clap,
each note that falls.

# *Darkly*

for Dave Smith

The moss never falls.
However gray,

it hangs like shirts
left to weather and rag

over the road
and the dead-end rail

and in all the branches
from there to the shore

and then as far upriver
as you can see.

Here it's only open water,
empty sky,

two ends of road no one uses,
landfill on one side, thicket

on the other,
the story of a bridge between.

Below, the water's huddled,
cold and silver.

It won't show a thing.
So I look for that place in the air

where they held a gun
on Willie Edwards

and told him he could jump.
*How* you'd ask me—

*Why?* so simple
it won't tell a thing—

how'd they get there,
Edwards in their hands,

along the roads so many others took
to church or to the movies

or home
along the same white lines?

To condemn is easy, you said,
to condemn is to turn away

where no one will ever understand.
So I go back, downtown,

to Jefferson Street, though
their haven, their Little Kitchen's gone.

I can cruise, can walk
and search each pane of glass

for that wave of heat,
the echo

that will fill the night
fifty years gone

when five men bent
in the diner's greasy light—

as Mongtomery darkened
beyond the window,

each bus offering its insult
or imagined slight—

and planned to kill a man
they'd never seen.

I can walk their streets,
though no one walks here anymore,

until I catch that curve
in a window or a windshield

that wrecks my face
so for a moment

I can mistake myself
for the redneck at the end of a joke.

Every map is open but a man,
and you can turn away

before you see how it's drawn,
or arrive too late

and miss that moment
when he sees himself as his language does,

when every other face
becomes the glass but his own.

Maybe the streetlamps remember the light,
gelid and thin as bacon fat,

as the vowel in your mouth
that just won't break,

a door I can walk through,
a room where I can sit beside them

hardly out of place,
then watch them rise and part

the city's yellow crape of light,
and then a door I can open

to follow through the warehouse streets
to the city's fence

with a memory
only half my own.

I know these nights.
The sky is ash

and if you wait too long
your bones sing in your fingers,

cold as galvanized wire.
The rest of the way

comes from somewhere else.
There are many ways to get there

and then the one
I can't understand:

already,
maybe always being there.

Maybe they were born
into that vacant sky

and they were always there,
ready to force a choice

so they wouldn't have to
make one,

waiting for someone else
to write their names in air or water.

They never arrived,
so it didn't matter

they'd grabbed the wrong man,
wouldn't have mattered

if they'd found the one
they were looking for.

They'd still disappear,
like the bridge,

and be forgotten by the water.
They'd still come,

each one, to that morning
at the end of everything

when they'd look back
on the healing water

and say
*My life hasn't meant a thing.*

Some things are beyond us.

The moss never falls.
The river won't say a thing.

I lean, clouding
its reflected night.

And now I can't tell you
how I got here

or what I'd hoped to see,
what face would rise

if light swept from the channel
or the opposite shore.

The sky is empty,
and the river's bent

like a question too close
or too far away to read.

# Narcissus incomparabilis

Lean down, lean down
while the light's abducted,
its last skirts caught
then torn through the trees.
Keep your own eye still
so no one catches you.
When it's gone, it's everywhere—
air a memory of light,
incident turned ambient,
and it never takes long
for this nacre to grow
over each absence or intruder
and become the world.
Lean down now,
creel of starlight and moon,
and reflect again
your inherited light.
World may ripple—
pearl, scale, pebble, bone—
behind all memory,
may ghost you, stranger,
where you don't belong.
But lean down now,
as memory hardens
its incomparable light.
Don't let the sun
set on you again.

# The Hands of Persons Unknown

Pearl River County, Mississippi, 1959–1960

Arrested for rape in February 1959, Mack Charles Parker was abducted from
jail and murdered on April 24, then recovered from the Pearl River May 4.
Grand juries, in November and January, wrote no indictment, and the case
was closed.

Ice buds on the oaks and hickories.
The rain, the ice keeps coming.
The limbs lean down. Light may stir
in the bulbs of ice then break, spread
and split in the smothering dark,
then close again, just headlamps passing,
ice cocooning every limb. Far ahead,
the husband stumbles toward town,
farther from the husking truck, no matter
what prays he will emerge.
At last what comes is a face, a gun,
a shatter. The trees lean down
their heavy fingers. Cold palps skin.

Rain hangs on the windows. Faint light
making eyes of the drops. Sleep is the scarf
pulled over your mouth, hair
curling on your neck, a dark path
through glistening woods. The eyes
gather light. A face arrives in the glass
to take you back, a hand at your back
that leads to a darkened room, a window
full of eyes, the sentences all the same.
Imagine them on the window's screen,
their ten eyes staring, the markings
they want you to name. The one that breaks
the silk and ice, the window. The night
exploding all around you again.

A gun, a net, a rope, a name
are offered. Again when you refuse.
An opening, an offering at every window.
At night you can lie awake, waiting
for moths to spread on the empty screen,
knowing they are moving in far counties of the dark,
how silk bruises then splits,
the plague of wings unholstered in quiet,
a silence you've refused to hear.
You can tell yourself it's just a dream
of ice, someone falling in the river,
not the sound of glass breaking miles away.

What's locked, what's wound will open.
A fist of keys can turn in a drawer,
fall out, fall open. What's braced
will loose and climb the stairs like a flood,
uncountable and sure. What keeps
will catch you, will say
*They've come for you* as if counties'
worth of water could claim its bed,
claim its crest in you. You leave
your mark, your water, but subside is slow,
a melt to the bridge, the bank, the stream,
high marks for a Bible and a brush
in the morning to wear it back again.

This is how they opened you:
a key, a stick, a chair,
a bullet to reach inside you,
a finger to curl from your heart
the ridicule that was theirs,
and one to ask the water
to do the rest. Now the river's taken you,
a gauze in every wound, a coil
in every coil and crease of skin, a pall
to draw you in the catfish dark
and pull your skin. This
is how they open you,
with sweat and rinse and breath,
a dozen counties' tributes
washing all around you.
And this is how they bury you,
their own ablutions slowly
cleaning out your wounds.

Now tell us how God put the heavens
from the earth, water from the earth,
how God drew the bounds we cannot undo.
Strain your voice above the crickets
and tell us how rain gathers
from towns of euphemism and prayer
*for whoever did this*, how rain gathers
from the eaves in Carthage and Philadelphia
and Jackson where the epithets hang.
Tell us how the river rises,
how one prayer becomes another
once it leaves the mouth.
Tell us how Mississippi
makes an undertaker of the water,
a perfect gauze for every wound.
Syllables worm in every hollow
of molest and decay and then withdraw.
How they callous the willow and the tung.

Break the finger open. Coil, whorl.
The mottle, the name that lies within.
*Mack Charles Parker,* missing.
Or the accident, *Charithonia,*
long wings pursing as the trees tell everything
to keep their quiet. The newsprint, the river,
the wind. The moon will not
indict the rope or the weight in the river's silt,
will not fall differently on the roofs
of confessors or confederates
or light the stumps of hanging trees
or the wrecks of cypresses where ivory-bills
fold one last time. It will stay, a finger
on the lips, then drain into the eddies
and the wake of whatever falls.

The year's last husks, crumpled notes
fall, not fast enough to be a snow.
Jury cards, summons. Transcript fragments.
Tung leaves between the live oaks
and cypresses where a chrysalis hangs
like a comma, skin beneath the nail.
But you are asked to keep secret
these proceedings. This you should
sacredly keep. Let the river
tongue its pearls, its ropes, what reflections
cast upon it. May this be the end.
Newspapers heron in the reeds,
pearlescent in half-light until the year
has turned. You are asked to keep this.
The last envelopes open slowly.
Caterpillars cut fingerprints in the leaves.

# A Natural History of Mississippi

A blade of rust from the ocean
and from the air a rumor
that corrodes the earth in tongues,
lichen, moss, magnolia,
until each gossip's true.
Things go this way,
each green repeating its fact
of sun and wind and rain,
its dialect, its blade,
while beneath each leaf
a quiet cuts between the veins.
Laced, pale wings open
to learn the particular weather,
the place or part of speech
that will darken
and give them a name.
So each sugar furls
to burn and bitter
against whatever mouths
might swallow,
each skin becomes
the history of its harbor,
another word for *here*.
This hatch of bark and shade
hangs like a photograph
of all it covers, so perfect,
so still, its edges
blur, then disappear.

# And Ever

for Medgar Evers
murdered June 12, 1963, Jackson, Mississippi

You rise
to watch the leaves

breathe light to their edges
and burn,

drawing day from the night
to wake the birds.

You've learned this sound,

white chord of a filling lung
that will set the wren to sing,

so you rise,
only today

it isn't leaves.
It's a moth you've never seen,

its wings
not flock, not felt,

but paper,

hundreds, thousands
of photographs

flickering in your breath
then falling,

each into its own light,
another pair of wings.

Now the windows switch,
Wallace incandescent

in the schoolhouse door,
Kennedy at his desk.

The children curl
in the broadcast's glow,

and beyond, silhouettes drift,
blotting fireflies from the night.

It hasn't rained for weeks,
and everyone is looking

for something to fall.

The airfield strobes planes
from the night.

Leaves pocket
the carhop's music.

And honeysuckle yawns
till everything smells like breath.

Dust settles
on the sleeping faces

as headlights sweep,
tires hush the drive.

As the moth on the window
folds to a bullet,

then unfolds
to watch again.

Then the light
is as fine as dust,

dust a moth strews
as it lights on the screen,

that falls on the face
like honeysuckle's musk.

Eyes flutter
the dust to angels

and the room
is a heaven,

throngs flocked
from the closet's sleeves

to the window
and out into the dim

where they hang
their trumpets in the vines.

They call through the crickets'
*ever* and *ever*,

then silk themselves
in question marks

beneath the leaves.

Or the light
is weak as a candle's,

swelling, then cooling
as you reach

for those unnamable wings.

Touch,
and they fan over the grass,

the yard's a writhe of flashlights,
fireflies when there shouldn't be,

dozens now luminous
in the fractured air.

Drift, shrivel,
they whet,

they hang themselves
in the honeysuckle

then bore deeper
into the leaves.

Fold back those wings,

the sleep they've gathered
in their eyes,

sleep that has forgotten you.

Fold back those wings
to a vial, a tablet,

lilac his shirt forgot.

The perfect sleeves,
the shirts you ironed

he said he wouldn't need.
The closet's furl

of empty arms—
fold back each one

until the shadow gutters
into the shoes,

into dust,
until you find

a breath
of yesterday's breath.

Somewhere here is an inch of cloth
light has not faded,

color not beaten white
by sun.

You look and then you're
gripping the sill

in that moment
when everything glows a little,

when the light is everywhere
and there are no shadows,

no matter how
you fold the curtain back.

⌢

The brother's face
at the airplane window.

And the dream again.
Willie Tingle,

their father's friend,
those hands,

broad day,
closing on his skin.

His face
as they bind him to the cart

and drag him
through Decatur's streets.

The field
where they tie him to a post.

His face
as they lash the shirt away.

As they tie the noose.
As they walk away.

They leave the shirt,
a shadow to outlive.

The hum of the body,

or its absence,
its sprawl.

The name
in the field he walks each day

with Medgar,
the only way to school.

Now he walks alone
through the damp clay of night

to watch moon soak
into the shirt's easing folds,

to watch moon crust
then flake into wings.

Light like a blind man's fingers
reading everything.

⌢

Then morning is dust
engrained in light's trajectories,

shirts that pollen
when you move.

Everything escapes us—

why we opened closets, doors,
what we said,

faces too bright to see.

Dust would settle
to flock the wings of touch,

lint would rise
if anyone was looking

when the shell is lifted,
the print peeled from the glass,

though to see is to know
everything as aftermath,

not the window
but the bore,

not the oil but the cotton
in the bullet's grooves,

plaque of light
on everyone's skin.

Soon the day will unfold its cruelties

and someone will have said
and someone will have written

*Maybe this will slow them down.*
Then everyone can read it,

and the bright faces
will fold like curtains

and leave you at the window
once again.

There,
the moth is spreading.

Lean close enough
and you can see

Medgar, fallen to the drive,
housekey in his outstretched hand.

Lean closer,
while the paper's turning,

while the light is bruising
to a dozen children caged in wire,

their fingers
all you see at first,

and then the dark equator
that halves their eyes,

the jagged latitude of pines

that swallows the last ash
and embers of the day.

Closer, now,

the weave of each child's shirt
is opening.

The cotton, the paper
swallow all the light.

⌢

And after day has staled
like a glass of water beside the bed,

after morning's gone,
what does anyone remember?

Nectar. Sweat.
The river's musk

neither a history
nor a promise of rain.

Honeysuckle's
the only breathing thing.

Children file with their flags
down the streets

and their flags are taken,
and they are taken,

from the street to the wagon,
from the wagon to the pen,

and the street is left to darken
the way the sky never will.

If anyone is missing
check the fairgrounds first,

check the cages they made
to hold them all.

Check the bushes and the vacant lots.
Someone ran away.

Something rustled in the vines
where they found the rifle

and a fingerprint so sweetgum-sharp
someone will know its tree.

Someone saw an empty car
in the drive-in lot,

the kind of white
that talks through the night to the moon.

The moon was failing and someone
turned as the TV cooled

to see the president's ghost
in the dimming tube.

A cab trawled the neighborhood,
a telegram or a passenger to unfold.

A man at the depot
read a phone book to the air,

and somewhere in the night
a radio played the speech again

and someone laughed
at *one hundred years of delay*

and someone stayed late
for the picture show.

And at the end when the ship was burning
and the theater filled with smoke,

a moth rose into the light
and came apart in the air.

Whatever falls
falls quietly

into the wool of breath,

into the handkerchief
or the sleeve.

An eyelash.
A tear.

Drops of sweat
to suggest the withheld rain.

And whatever falls
falls through the temple's boiling air,

switch of paper fans
and photographs

and the strobes
that hold your face a moment,

*first one cheek,*
        *then the other . . .*

And whatever falls
falls quietly

into the eulogy
he hadn't wanted

because *those who give them*
*never mean them,*

into the newsreels' whispers,

into the scent of gladiolas
and the stink of film

which is the smell of memory
as it leaves you,

given like a pollen.
Its flowers

write themselves
into your fingers

and become a part of everything
you touch.

The arms that hold you
when you leave the temple,

the hands,
the crowded air.

What follows is the sound
of song choked back,

forbidden hymn
that needs to break

like glass on the asphalt
and give back the day.

What follows is the hush of cloth,
the silent march

down Lynch Street
and across the tracks

where policemen thicken
on the white side of town,

then Farish
where every window

is a book of eyes,
faces, noise.

Crewcut teens and jukebox blare
in a drugstore's door

till someone pulls the plug

so the wish of pants legs and skirts
can fill the street again.

Later the song will break,
one voice, then another,

*this little light of mine,*
then dozens, hundreds running

*all over Capitol Street,*
*I'm gonna let it shine*

on the riot squad's
bright helmets.

And later, the man in the paper
with a bandaged skull

and a shirt torn to gauze,
a room of song behind him,

will be pulled from a building
and beaten again

and thrown in the fairgrounds' cages
with trucks of other mourners.

But for now his is just one of the faces
waiting as the coffin's drawn

into the funeral home,
where the wood is polished,

where the flag is tucked
for the ride to Washington,

just one of the faces
the bearers can see

through the curtains,
the shirt

just one of thousands
now blistering in the sun.

⌢

They're waiting in their Sunday bests
when the hearse arrives,

knowing somehow
he would be coming,

crowding the platform
when the caisson rolls into the frame

with the flag-draped coffin,
turned away

toward the schedule
that tells how long they have.

When the train is boarded,
they crowd the window

where the women sit
with the flag,

and as the station pulls away,
as town gives way

to field, even in the thickets
they're there—their shirts,

their hats and dresses
flowering the blur—

and in Tuscaloosa
and Birmingham and Anniston,

turning the stations into churches,
knowing somehow he would be coming.

46

Whenever they wake,
they are there—

impossible to see them all,

waiting like water
in the trampled fields,

like shards of moon
in the evening's failures,

glass that gathers
the fugitive light.

And even now.

As dust lays its unclosable wings
on the faces of the sleeping,

as it settles into the breath
and the tangles of vine,

the window's bore,
the kitchen's pale seizures of light—

even now,
as she looks again,

glowing soft as honeysuckle's lamps,
as moths against the glass.

# Mothlight

after Stan Brakhage

Lace your fingers, your hands
    on your stomach like the hands
of the dead, though yours rise
    on your breath. In sleep
they fall away. You wake,
    a knuckle on the floor,
one finger weiring the dust,
    the sprawl of human skin.

In sleep they fall away,
    your hands, they cover the floor,
the sifted skin on every board
    now glowing like a varnish,
like resin in the early light,
    and sleep is the fog
in which you've spread your touch,
    the dream of feeling everything.

Each board from the bed
    to the window and the television
where you've watched moths rise
    to the fingertip of the streetlamp
and the apparitions of the news,
    where they've battered the glass
and the screen into their moment's haloes,
    the dust that spreads the light.

It falls back like your hands,
    like those moths now folded

dark beneath the screens. Can you feel them
    in the flat of your forsaken hand?
Their quiet a dream of quiet,
    a sleep no word can break. Can you
lift them to the window's scrim,
    that paper, that dust, these ellipses

of light? Raise them to the day
    and let them fall, through themselves,
again. Then mark where they lie,
    each a frame of arrested flight.
Then begin, with invisible ribbon,
    with resin, and lay them end to end,
end to end, again—how many?—
    until this stillness moves.

# Collect

... in a way, all of us are responsible for Bo's death, because we've let people like those killers have their way, and decent people have just sat by.

—Mamie Till, 1956

Morning wraps the stars and the dark
that will come again

and so is a promise,
an envelope

in which some dark may be folded
like a list of names,

so first light on the Tallahatchie
is a prayer that light

may be shoaled
by some arm or shoulder

as a pane of light will smoke
until the swollen face emerges

and morning on a magazine's spread
burns into the retinas

the letters of a prayer for the river
and the pine box and the boxcar

on which some light no one will ever remember
has already laid its blessing

and a prayer for Mamie Till
for looking when they told her not to,

for leaving the casket open
so everyone could see

what hatred can do to a body,
what color can do,

so Chicago's breath could settle
through the glass and the suit and into the wounds

to be taken back into the lungs,
a gauze to blot astonishment,

so Mississippi's breath, stolen north,
could swathe him too

then gather like river in our lungs
and keep some part of breath

from entering there again
and so become a prayer

for the breath we did not take
for the words we did not say,

the missing part of breath that makes a silence
in which a body can break the water's calm,

in which everything can be heard,
light peeling from the wounds of the stars

and distant birds that sing like glass,
a clot in the tissue of the sky.

**TWO**

# City of Grace

Welcome to Jackson: City of Grace and Benevolence

City of Grace, you open,
you part your curtains
and smile like a hostess
when we call your name,
you tender what any traveler needs,
a call to ease, a balm,
a kindness, whatever storm.
You take us in. City of Grace
and Benevolence, you say
you know what solace means,
burned so often they called you
Chimneyville, and now
you can't forget,
you've written it in bronze
outside the City Hall
the War made a hospital
for the Yankee
and for your Rebel sons,
like the one who is always dying
outside the Capitol.
City of Fame,
you hold him still, laurel
on your crown, fan
making a hand of wind
to soothe his face
and fill the eagle's wings
spread above to promise,
*Virtute et armis*, to say again
just how far you'll go.
City of Remembrance,
you keep so well, you show us
where Welty lived,

the house still there, how she skated
to the library, through
the Capitol, the book
now cast and open in her hands.
Tell me now, City of Embrace,
of the newsreels' children
rounded from their march,
flags gathered, the children
trucked to the fairground cages,
the ones who peer out
through the chicken wire.
City of Richard Wright
and Ross Barnett, tell me
not just where the Governor pled
*I love Mississippi, I love her people,*
*her customs,* but where the writer
went to school, a short walk
from here, thinking *it was not*
*until one wanted the world to be different*
*that one would look at the world*
*with will and emotion,* and tell me,
then, where Medgar Evers lived,
whom you remember
with a post office and a stamp
and an airport, though
when I've asked you've turned
to someone else and said
*Can you help this man find his friend?*


\*


Ambivalent City, you know the way,
but you let me find it, the statue,
the library, miles away,
the Boulevard, and then the house,
the plaque that tells us

this is where he lived, perfect
as a photograph, as a movie,
only the color's unreal,
or too real, the green piercing,
the hose uncoiled as if someone
might return to water the lawn.
Neighbors cruise, panning
like cameras as I stand
where he must have stood
choosing the house with no front door,
where Beckwith must have stood,
who drove the town asking everyone
where Evers lived, where
he marked his man.
There is nowhere else to stand.
A city is a kind of memory,
and if you stay too long
the shape of someone else
will hold you there
until day repeats its failure
and the streetlights wake
and yawn all color from the dusk
and the house becomes a photograph
of itself and the small wings
unfold from the fabric of night,
from all the magnolias' ears
and the broad stretch of the reservoir
and the river you can smell
as they gather into pearls
the stars' historic light,
the eyes' whose looking stays
long after the pupils
have burned away. Fireflies
fall back into the grass,
and the mayflies clasp each other
in a kind of halo. City of Ghosts,
you can't abandon your history,

and it won't abandon you.
You watch each other,
you call each other's names.
The sidewalks, the driveways
gleam like quarried moon,
and each open hand repeats
the ambient light as the crickets
fill with heat and raise again
the street's last breath:
*Turn me loose.*

# Self-Portrait as a Moment in 1963

Supper's late, and my mother sprawls
before the console, half-watching *Gunsmoke*,

Alabama History spread before her,
though school's almost out for summer

and the chicken's almost fried
to that perfect crisp. Then it's over,

credits stamped over final stills,
and the show gives way to news,

a minute of film from Birmingham,
not an hour south, where police

are turning dogs on kids as young
as she, spraying them with hoses

until they fall, the water she isn't watching
curling like smoke in the air.

My grandmother flicks the switch
and they're gone. They eat

in quiet, each cutting a breast
or thigh into steam, forking

beans or macaroni until
the plates' blank faces shine again.

This is years before
she'd meet my father, before

I'd come to that table,
that food, that room.

There's a silence here
I want to scratch away

so I can see what's underneath,
what they don't recall.

I want to turn someone's head,
my grandfather's maybe, or my mother's,

back toward the TV, where
the tube's still fading,

the ghost of that scene
on the edge of that room.

I want someone there to see
and remember, so I can leave

and go back into the future,
not history. Not yet.

# Before Knowing Remembers

Oxford, Mississippi

Day pulls back into its sleeves,
        slipping its fingers from the banisters
and door handles. It's going now

like a drunk, erratic, slow,
        losing itself in the trees,
leaving us in shadow on the Square

where the stone Confederate
        keeps my eye. Imagine
always walking over the open earth,

coming back alone, snuggling
        nights in a ditch
and piling the leaves over you

to bank your fire. If I
        could reach him now, I'm sure
I'd feel the chill, his boots

cold as another beer. I'm waiting
        for the cool on a barroom balcony,
half-listening while someone else

is talking about our Johnny Reb,
        just one of thousands, she says,
if the story can be believed,

North and South, same stance,
        same molded face—
*only their hats are different*

she says, as if to say, don't believe
                    it all, Mississippi of butternut
and cotton, though even that,

the caution's local, a conversation
                    that won't be happening
in too many other towns.

Her companion's all linen and buff
                    and sharp Van Dyke,
but for the neck tattoo

a fair portrait of General Lee.
                    Another studied irony.
I can see him in a reenactor's jacket

cranking a strat through some Delta blues,
                    and I realize that's what he wants,
what we all want, anything

to keep history on the move,
                    so we can be Americans,
or just the kind of Southerners

we think we ought to be.
                    Behind them, just inside
the doors, Robert Johnson's muraled

in his midnight meet, Satan
                    either imminent
or already gone. The only way

to know is to look past
                    that graveyard of a smile
and down the throat, to find

the cradle of song either empty
               or aflame.
The mouth is open

and you know that music,
               but you can't hear a thing.


                    *


Mississippi's thumping now
               the way you do
after five rounds, or six,

the cast-iron night
               rank as guitar strings
coiled in sweat. Two doors down,

a hill-country trio's set
               to work it all night long,
their blues insistent, entrancing.

Slowly, you're drawn
               into that pulse,
down the stairs, then pulled into

some mercantile's upper room,
               now stomped into a juke,
where skin touches skin

and every song's a weave of limbs
               no one owns. Sweet amnesia
of smoke and beer, a fire

that burns, a cup that cools,
               that room is a heaven
where heat forgets the sun,

where legs forget their walking
　　　　down a road or a row
of cotton or acres and acres

of ornamental lawns, where
　　　　you can forget that posture,
those words, that weight,

a lecture hall with a window
　　　　on the ground where
the newsman lay, the Frenchman

with a bullet in his back
　　　　and a black rope of blood
to tie him to the night

while the hurry just passes by,
　　　　a rush of arms and faces
who will take your pain.

Holler and strobe, we come together
　　　　in a downtown room,
through a door anyone can take

into this prayer-meeting warmth
　　　　though no one's asked
which god it's for. It's September

and we're dancing, everyone
　　　　is dancing, and this
is how a town forgets,

by becoming what it didn't want
　　　　to be. You take
what's offered, you give the same,

a neck ready for someone's arms,
          someone else's warmth still
in the sleeves. Slowly you're carried,

breath and pulse and flesh,
          out into the night,
where the courthouse and its soldier

bask in their halogens, the magnolias
          and sidewalks slick
with rain, the light

nervous on your skin. On the pavement
          the water's gathering
to rise like tear-gas,

steam's rags regular as the riff
          you still hear, pulled apart
in the bluesman's hands, hands

old enough to know that night,
          decades back, and the other,
the juke-box repairman

shot dead in the campus riot,
          then slid back together,
that time infallible and perpetual

through the vapor, the smoke.
          Part of you must still be there
in that room, just waiting

for him to catch your eye
          through the brawl, and now
he does, raising his pick hand

into a pistol, and then
        he cocks the thumb
and points it right at you.


*


The music never stops,
        never really goes away,
but people fall back into themselves

and leave, walking away
        through the fog, toward campus
or the cemetery or sleepier streets.

They're mostly silhouettes,
        densities in the powdery light.
I'm watching next to Faulkner's

bronze, on the bench
        that replaced the one he kept
each afternoon, where he marked

the county's comings and goings,
        but now the Square's
as much like a *Life* magazine

as *Light in August*, and I think
        this is how a town remembers,
when no one's looking

but the statues, the soldier
        and the writer
who must have seen it coming,

who knew how two people
        can struggle in a body,
a house, a town, and how a place

won't recognize itself
             until the story's nearly over.
That night,

before the first gun was pulled,
             before the first window
broke, Meredith

was already there, sleeping
             in a dorm in a vacant part
of campus, the half-exhausted

light barely touching him.
             He slept well, he says.
He didn't hear a thing.

They are all sleeping now,
             all of them, in houses
like these, becoming pictures

of themselves, street-light sepia
             and salted pale,
or downhill in St. Peter's, beneath

their pillars and stones.
             All night, people come
to leave their roses

or pour whiskey into the letters
             of someone else's name,
leaving that smell in the crape

of the cedar trees. And sometimes
             a mockingbird will wake
from the solid calm and spill

whatever it's heard, as if
        it gathered what's mumbled
in dreams and now

it's giving everything back to the air
        and the streetlamps if it goes on
long enough, and the world starts

moving again, wrens and robins
        and all the rest, the houses
coalescing from the dark.

Each night, we drift,
        we are taken out of ourselves
and we forget, until

something like this
        puts us back in a sentence
or a story of the world,

in a quiet room or a graveyard
        where none of the names
are ours again,

where the light reaches slowly
        out of itself and wakes us,
like a hand on our hands,

remembered warmth
        on our skin.

# The Second Person

Natchez

Afternoon burns everything off Franklin Street.
    Even the birds, even the flies.

Or iced-tea sugar and chicken grease weigh everyone
    into a doze, all indoors, in a cool

they said would never come eighty years ago
    when this was still the center of business

and the civilized left these high hours to the dogs,
    ice in a highball, and let each house

close its lids a while. They've kept their quiet,
    so I'm alone before the windows,

the radiant panes, each with its scrim of clay,
    the finish the river gives everything,

so nothing, not even glass, is clear.
    It's almost painful, this saturation,

this street and its stores of rugs and signs and flags,
    bright and strange as a magazine photo

you'd find in an attic or an antique store,
    hard to believe the color was ever real.

The teacups, the painted china and jeweled eggs,
    even the bottles, medicine vials

and flasks each with its ounce of dirt,
    even the smell of the prolific earth,

the sedimentary atmosphere of empire chairs
        and oak armoires and mantles that survive

their tall, white homes, like the plantation house
        where, later, I'll witness again

the marriage of gray suit and hoop skirt
        that still feels like a dream, where I'll walk

out of—or is it into?—myself,
        the maitre'd's small, solicitous voice

proffering another julep—cotton-leaf hand,
        silver cup—though even he must be

a reenactment or a revenant,
        a hanger for the clothes of memory.

I will take it, I would, a handful of refuge
        in unthinking weather, will take

the same lethargic joy in a breeze, any chill
        in the throat, any kind of shade—

so I enter the dim of one old cotton house,
        its air-conditioned maze of hand-tools

and quilts, corn cribs and cotton gins, and of course
        the owner's smile, porcelain, bright, almost

blinding, blooming in welcome and how-you-do
        and what-brings-you. We talk amid rows

of cook-stoves, stew-pots, and cast-iron skillets
        about the wedding I've come to see

on the famed estate, the time the town exploded,
        the Rhythm Club's inferno, and then

she ventures she knows the accent, knows
        I'm from Alabama, and soon she's eloquent

on our lakes and rivers, where the mister takes her
        every chance they get. She's seen it all,

so she asks where I'm from, and when I say
        she starts to glow, gushing over mountains

all the way to Gatlinburg. She's walked each one,
        even skied the state's one slope, which conjures

not the "Southern snow" that required almost everything
        around us, but snow, cold snow, a thought

that cools me further, so my sweat is nearly dry
        when the smile tightens across her teeth

and she leans in to say *I just love it*
        *you know—there are no darkies there.*

Then afternoon is a conspiracy of color,
        an echo the heat or the history

in our voices draws us into—
        someone else's version of ourselves—

and the inevitable, painful quiet
        in which an answer must arrive.

What can you say? And how long do you have to wait
        before you can leave, before you can walk

out of yourself and down the cotton-trading streets
　　　　into the smother of trees

on some more recent lane? How long do you have to wait
　　　　before you can leave and not be followed,

and how long do you have to walk before the mockingbirds
　　　　drown in bass and drum and anger,

before you can cross back into the proper century?
　　　　The smell of the river stays with you,

maybe even grows as you move so you don't know
　　　　where you're going, and the key in your hand

could open a car door or a plantation room
　　　　or nothing at all, some door that's vanished

in the air, June's shimmer from the asphalt
　　　　and the roofs of every house, so you walk

toward that moment when the sun starts burning
　　　　and the magnolias' thick perfume washes

all around and you find yourself on a corner,
　　　　all linen and sweat, again the only one

who'd walk in a heat like this. You have no idea
　　　　where you are, so you cock your head

as if you might hear your way through the afternoon,
　　　　and when you raise your head, you see,

across the street, two men hunched in shadow
　　　　on a barbershop's stoop, ties

dangling like smoke in the solid air. They've seen you
 and now their brows sharpen

as if they know, too, you're not from here,
 and in the space between you anything

could pass, the ghosts of Farragut or Grant
 or a hot white Caddy rattling New Orleans Bounce,

you're waiting to see, it seems like years or centuries,
 then one rises, ties his tie, and steps back in,

leaving the other, who keeps your eye
 a moment longer then looks into the distance

through that lace of smoke that seems etched in the air
 for something far behind you, something

you don't even know how to look for,
 something that may never arrive.

# Self-Portrait in a Plate-Glass Window

Selma

Steam rises from my plate,
        chicken and greens and black-eyed peas,

and in the window where I can look
        beneath the honeydew rind or sliver moon of scalp

through my own reflected eyes
        to the sidewalk and the lot beyond

then back to the dim interior where the owner
        turns from his TV mystery back to me.

It's the right address,
        though the name has changed,

and he must be asking, as I am,
        am I where I'm supposed to be?

A few doors up—I can almost see it—
        a plaque remembers

James Reeb, the reverend, who'd come to march
        and last ate in this café.

It was Walker's, then.
        Klansmen watched across the street,

waiting for the collar, for the face to emerge—
        three of them, maybe four,

with pipes and bats in the door of a grocery
        someone demolished years ago.

Eyes down, I'm working to the blank plate
            and the questions that have to follow—

*Where you from? What you after?*—
            even if no one says a thing.

The quiet holds them the way
            dark will hold all color

and one memory will look like another
            and staying will seem stranger than having come.

We'll rise, then, the glass between us,
            one in the dusk, one inside,

close enough to feel the café's warmth
            radiating into the town

and the cool March evening
            reaching into the room.

We'll walk toward the door
            and become one

and slide off the glass,
            leaving only the window

with its inscription
            of moonlight and clouds

tomorrow will rub
            almost entirely away.

# Self-Portrait at a Bend in the Road

Tarsus, Alabama

It takes a while to find the place
        where I can hold the photograph
and the mountain will finish itself,

and a while until I'll let it drop,
        unafraid that the bus will be there
evaporating into flame,

the mob still shouting, still waiting
        for the troopers and agents to clear
so they can finish the job,

or the Freedom Riders they've chased
        from Anniston, still
smoked out and choking on the grass.

So much else is gone—
        the grocery where the driver ran
"for help," the homes

where Mother's Day dinners cooled
        while the locals watched the smoke
agitate the north Alabama sky,

and Janey Miller, the twelve year old
        with a well bucket
and a dipper for anyone who coughed.

They taunted her, her neighbors,
        the store owner and the riot,
even the bus driver safe within the fold,

but she carried on,
        and they carried on,
even after the wreck was towed,

until the Millers packed and were gone.
        But half of that, maybe more,
would be torn down to widen the road,

and that silence would be lost,
        would be written over,
leaving the road a by-way, a dead end

with a plaque where people
        hold photographs to the air
so they can stand where the newsmen stood,

over that place where the Riders waited
        in a circle of grace and disbelief,
fragile as the surface of a ladle

that hears each word.
        Now the traffic's talking over
something else, I catch myself

on the car's hot windows,
        distorted just enough
to be someone else—a cousin

or a local on the edge of the frame
        ready to disappear
into the smoke or the heat or the trees.

The mountain's dark behind me.
        My hand's on the latch,
the last warmth still there.

One of us is leaving.

One of us is already gone.

# Shore

Aaron Lee, June 12, 1967, New Orleans
Joseph Thomas, September 9, 1967, New Orleans


Here you are only epitaphs,
only names, dates

on the list I carry and unfold
when the light seems quiet enough.

You are just this spill of a city,
no ward, no neighborhood, as if

that last place can't be touched,
as if the line had slipped

through some scar the water multiplied
then forgot. That water's

everywhere, reaching through the trees,
in the steam of afternoon,

the smell of everything,
and that tremble in it,

the afterward of that last reflection.
Somewhere you are burned

on an inch of film—your names,
your faces, maybe your last addresses,

places where I could ask again—
so the reels unwind

in a library's dim, old bulbs'
dirty light scumming the emulsion's

oil, that chemical sprawl,
that rainbow

the dead always leave behind.

Aaron Lee, you are a forgotten mile
in New Orleans East,

an alleyway of scrapyards and boxcars
and derelict homes, trailer parks

now laced as curtains
where the flood has grazed,

a place even the maps might forget.
The water stays—

between the lilies and the cattails' blades,
between the gravel knuckles

in the tar—the water stays,
keeping that place

you last touched the earth,
where you rose up,

Biblical, in air
before gravity remembered you

and called you home again.
And now it keeps the rest,

the car that launched you,
that drove away, the friend

thrown too, into the reeds,
and even the house,

just west of here, where
you'd never arrive,

abandoned as a name
no one answers to.

And you, Joseph Thomas,
you are an empty lot,

a field behind a chain-link fence
where the St. Bernard Project

used to be, where one night
you walked into the yard

and slumped into the grass
as if sleep suddenly found you

and you collapsed under its weight
and lay down where the dew

would cover you. Hours later,
someone would pull back

that blanket and find you cold,
your last breath gelled

in your philtrum, inarticulate
ink the bullet spilled.

Hours later, someone
would turn you over

in that yard which is not here anymore
in this field between Hamburg and Gibson

that has forgotten everything
but a single tree—

each doorway, each window,
each lot-line and walkway,

even that place
where the sniper stood,

which could be
right where I'm standing now.

There are no answers.
There is no one to ask.

An ice-cream truck sings its way
down Gentilly's abandoned mile

and three bulldozers ply
St. Bernard's vacant ground,

but no one stops,
and downtown, where the smell

of the river's even stronger,
a librarian files the reels again

and the steel drawers
click shut.

I have little more
to write beside your names

on this list of martyrs,
of people to be pulled back

through the glass of history,
this list where you stand

for everyone who had a killing
but not a killer,

for everyone who simply disappeared,
who walked out

as if into air, taken
in a fog's unknown hands,

leaving nothing but a name,
a date, and that fear,

constant as water,
that anyone could be next.

I fold the page again
and peel my shoes from the mud.

Everything smells, as it always did,
of mud, of river and lake

and live oak. Everything's reaching up
like that one great hand

in the middle of the rubbled lots,
like the fingers of the sago

in a ditch on the edge of town,
the way it always does,

trying to hold something
that might rise and be gone.

Wherever you touch the earth,
it can grab at your heels,

and you can look back
at the wells your walking's made

and watch as the water touches,
then fills them in.

# Self-Portrait in the Town Where I Was Born

West Palm Beach, Florida

The smell of the ocean,
the brine, must be

the first smell,
the smell of beginning.

Age is everything else.
Fish and skin,

asphalt and gasoline
volatile as moonshine in the heat,

a shower's galvanized water
peppering the air

and the ash of a campfire
the tide's raked out,

thin sugar of beer
and a tea of flotsam and bait

a wave could strew on the sand
and return to claim again.

A child climbs from the surf,
and we walk away.

We drive with the windows down,
beach and its high-rise barrier behind,

Belle Glade and Okeechobee
beyond the low storm of pines,

when the tang of hickory snares us,
pulls us over the tracks

and past the liquor store
to a squat block front,

its yard a wreck
of stumps and logs.

Inside, the menu's compendious—
conch, shrimp, crab—

and vinegar sharpens the air,
so strong for once

we forget the ocean.
We wait, almost alone.

A girl sits, opposite us,
baby on her shoulder.

As pitmen shout behind the counter,
as cleavers fall,

she watches us.
And then she asks

*What y'all doing here?*

The knives are moving,
but it seems quiet,

and I almost answer
*I was born here,*

almost say we came
to find that first place,

or we were lost
when we caught the smell,

or we were hungry
and someone showed us here.

But this is a question
of contrast, not motive.

This is the moment
we become visible,

when we emerge or develop,
the only whites in a block or two.

What would the camera see?
Wood paneling behind us,

wall sawed open for another AC,
sauce-red paint on all the sills,

peeling in the salt and breeze,
and someone,

there,
on the edge of the frame,

leaning on a car, as if watching
or talking back to me.

It's late,
and now everyone is watching,

waiting as I take a breath—
vinegar and brine

in the rising wind—
everyone waiting

for the sound I'll make,
the first word I'll say.

# Elegy

Gadsden, Alabama

The finger is gone that pointed the way
      so the General could escape,
the Confederate who would enshrine the finger
      and its girl and turn them into stone,
and now the finger is gone from the marble hand,
      proving every body is mutable,
however white, so the finger is just a story
      of a finger that points to its absence
which everyone ignores as they pass
      incognito as the getaways
of suburban legend, having gloved the hand
      and hung until it gave
so they could move like Forrest
      away from the water and into history,
lost in the crowd or the trees, until that day
      after each Thanksgiving
when all the county's majorettes, its quarterbacks
      and former mayors and fez-hatted shriners
file in their large white Cadillacs,
      those heroes among them, waving
as they pass down Broad Street, disappearing
      as if she still pointed the way.
They don't look back. Behind her the bridge
      arches over the compendious river,
into the dimmer streets of East Gadsden
      where, one parade night, two men
knocked then shot a preacher in his door,
      sure of a Black Panther front—a fist
they had to keep from rising—then pulled away,
      slowly, as if in their own parade,

these Klansmen, Forrest's distant kin,
　　　　scanning the windows and the doors,
passing the boarded juke and the store
　　　　where months later a neighborhood teen
would rob and hold the clerk at gunpoint
　　　　and push him into the storeroom
and douse him in gasoline then light the match
　　　　*just to scare him*, he'd say,
before the flames went up, burning his face
　　　　into a map of the county everyone would read
as an answer, leaving him to stagger,
　　　　leaving him to crawl toward the door
to call out through the slow bleed of dawn.

In Greek, *elegy* means *mourning song*,
　　　　a poem for what's been lost, and the Greeks
always cut something from their lines,
　　　　a syllable or two, to create a silence
or a place to hear it, maybe breaking meter
　　　　and slipping in an *iamb*, which means *limping*
or *lame*, like the gait of a wounded man,
　　　　stepping quick then stopping, so the pain can arrive,
and so the elegy, the mourning song,
　　　　reaches for what's missing or left behind,
like the woman who found the preacher
　　　　gasping in his door,
or the one who knelt beside the clerk
　　　　on the banks of a silence she could not ford,
or like the teenager, or like the finger,
　　　　or the fist it leaves behind as if to say
even memory can forget itself
　　　　and be written into another history
while everyone is looking at something else.
　　　　The Caddies slide into the night
and are folded once again beneath their hoods.

The cheerleaders, the shriners, and the quarterbacks
take off their suits and enter the crowds again,
        and we drive through those streets
where the night, where the day falls
        as indifferently as before.
We come over the bridge.
        We do not look back.
We think of the girl as we pass,
        and the finger we imagine still pointing the way.

# Notes

### On *Persons Unknown*

The present volume extends a series of poems dedicated to the memories of the martyrs of the Civil Rights movement, forty of whose names are inscribed on the stone table of the Civil Rights Memorial in Montgomery, Alabama.

In the broadening conversation about the Civil Rights movement, racial violence, hate crimes, and unsolved murders, more than eighty additional martyrs have been identified.

As that conversation expands, so does this project.

I have endeavored to link this body of work to the previous volume *A Murmuration of Starlings* (Southern Illinois University Press, 2008). The reader is invited to take this book, to split it between the first and second sections, and to insert the first section of *Persons Unknown* into the text of *A Murmuration of Starlings* before its central poem, "Tuck"; and to insert the second section of *Persons Unknown* into the text of *A Murmuration of Starlings* after the poem "Tuck" but before "For Reverend James Reeb."

### Sources and Debts

In constructing these poems, I have engaged in a great deal of research—traditional library research, which involves a number of books, newspaper articles, and the like; cultural research, which has drawn music, film, and television into the aperture of the work; and physical (if not forensic) research, which involves traveling to the locales of the murders. There are therefore many sources, some I will have forgotten to name, and some so broad they can only be indicated by the name of a city, county, or parish.

"Homochitto"—David Ridgen, *Mississippi Cold Case.*
"Sensitivity"—Charles Mingus, *Mingus Ah Um*; Brian Priestly, *Charles Mingus.*
"Darkly"—City of Montgomery, Alabama.
"The Hands of Persons Unknown"—Howard Smead, *Blood Justice*; City of
    Poplarville, Mississippi; *Poplarville Democrat*; Poplarville Public Library.
"And Ever"—Myrlie Evers, *For Us the Living*; Willie Morris, *Ghosts of Medgar Evers*; Reid Massengill, *Portrait of a Racist*; Adam Noisetter, *Of Long Memory*; Maryann Vollers, *Ghosts of Mississippi*; Rob Reiner, *Ghosts of Mississippi.*

"Mothlight"—Stan Brakhage, *Mothlight.*

"Collect"—Christopher Mettress, *The Lynching of Emmett Till: A Documentary History.*

"City of Grace"—City of Jackson, Mississippi; Richard Wright, *Black Boy.*

"Before Knowing Remembers"—William Faulkner, *Light in August*; City Grocery; City of Oxford, Mississippi; Junior Kimbrough, *All Night Long.*

"The Second Person"—City of Natchez, Mississippi; Natchez Public Library.

"Self-Portrait in a Plate-Glass Window"—City of Selma, Alabama; Town's Café.

"Self-Portrait at a Bend in the Road"—City of Anniston, Alabama; Raymond Arsenault, *Freedom Riders*; Town of Bynum, Alabama; Town of Tarsus, Alabama; with thanks to Harvey Jackson.

"Shore"—City of New Orleans; New Orleans Public Library.

"Self-Portrait in the Town Where I Was Born"—City of Riviera Beach, Florida, and McCrary's Barbecue; City of West Palm Beach, Florida.

"Elegy"—City of Gadsden, Alabama; *Bruce Botsford v. State of Alabama* (309 S0.2d 835, 54 Ala.App. 482; 7 Div 309); thanks to Tim St. John, Natasha Trethewey, and Carol Roark York.

With special thanks to Susan Glisson, Charles Centerfeit Hart, and Tom Freeland.

# Other Books in the Crab Orchard Series in Poetry